I Remember When:
The Untold Story of Helen Ellett

Randy Kneer

Randy Kneer
Typing and Editing: Diane Seaver
Editor: David Hayden
First Edition 2011

Published by
Podskoch Press, Ltd.
43 O'Neill Lane,
East Hampton, Connecticut 06424

podskoch@comcast.net
www.firetowerstories.com
www.adirondackstories.com
www.cccstories.com
www.firelookout.org

Copyright 2011 © by Randy Kneer
All rights reserved under International and Pan-American Copyright Conventions.
No part of this publication may be reproduced or transmitted
without consent in writing from the publisher.

ISBN 978-0-9794979-3-3

Manufactured in the United States of America

6 5 4 3 2 1
Cover illustration by Lindsay Baker
Maps by Paul Hartmann
Ford Folios Inc.

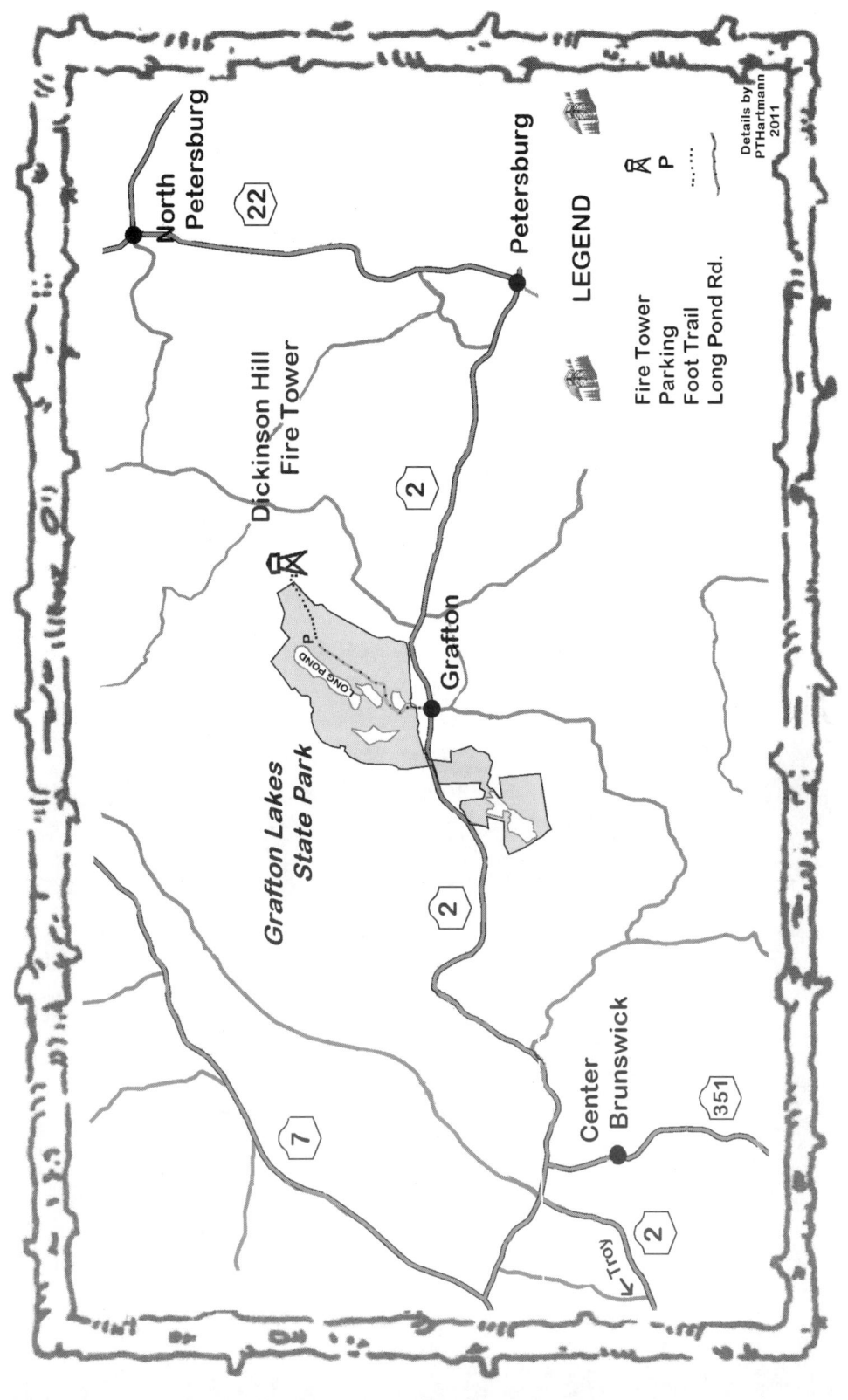

Introduction

I have known Randy for a long time. He has been a part of our custodial staff at Tamarac Elementary for many years. Oftentimes, Randy would stop by at the end of the day just to chat.

One day in March of 2010, Randy started talking about this book that he was writing. He explained how he had been interviewing Helen Ellett. At one time, she was a fire observer in the Grafton Hill Fire Tower. His short clips of her story were very intriguing. Before I knew it, I found myself offering to help him with the editing and typing. I told Randy that we needed to set a goal of finishing the book by September. Also, I needed him to start transcribing his conversations with Helen so I could start editing the story right away. In April, Randy stopped by my classroom with a notebook that had twenty pages of handwritten material. He was beaming from ear to ear. He couldn't wait to read to me some of his favorite parts.

As I started editing, I realized that I needed to meet Helen. We set up a time for a visit. It was delightful to meet Helen and her daughter Connie. We spent the whole afternoon sharing stories.

Diane Seaver

Later that day, Randy brought me up into the tower so I could get a better feel for what Helen experienced. The view was spectacular. You could see the different mountain ranges for miles. Randy explained how the scenery had changed over time. Many of the trees had grown up making it harder to identify specific places. Also, I was taken aback by the size of the cab. It was incredibly small. The platform is only about 7' by 7'. I struggled to believe how Helen could enjoy her long hours up in the tower, but she claimed it was the best job that any woman could ever want.

As time went on, Randy periodically gave me more handwritten pages. Each new group of pages brought about more questions for Helen. We planned another visit and had a glorious time. She and Connie are so easygoing and fun to be with. It was like we had been friends for years.

After I had finished editing the first draft, Randy brought the story to Helen and her family. Now it was time for them to critique the details to assure that they were correct. Changes definitely had to be made which allowed for another visit and a time to hear more stories. Helen always had another story to tell. And of course, it had to be added into the manuscript.

Then came the time to present the story to the publisher, Marty Podskoch. Randy and I were a little nervous for we didn't know what type of changes would have to be made. We were delighted to hear that Marty was pleased.

Later, Randy told me that both the publisher and his editor wanted to meet Helen and Connie. We set up another visit, had lunch, shared more stories and discussed which pictures would be put into the book. The afternoon went by quickly and everyone had a wonderful time.

Overall, this has been a very special experience. Helping Randy with his book, meeting Helen and Connie, and visiting the tower are memories that I'll cherish forever.

Preface

It all began on November 6, 2008 when Marty Podskoch was doing a slide show presentation at Tamarac Elementary School to the fourth and fifth grade class. During that presentation on the fire towers of the Adirondacks, Marty had included a picture of Helen Ellett at her tower in the 1940s gazing out, looking for signs of smoke. Marty turned to me and said in front of the whole class: "We are trying to see if Randy can do a story on Helen." I was stunned by his comment. I knew a lot about Helen but I never saw myself as an author. So, I dismissed the thought of writing a book.

Later that day, Marty was scheduled to present a slide show on the CCC camps at the Grafton Inn. It was for the Friends of Grafton Lakes State Park Annual Dinner Meeting. I was the president of the group. Marty and I had about two hours of free time before we headed off to the inn, so we went to Anthony's Pizza Restaurant across from the school to have something to eat. As I sat at the table with Marty, I said: "Helen Ellett is coming to the show tonight at the Grafton Inn. I asked her last week if she wanted to come and she said: 'Yes.'" I remember that conversation with her very clearly because she started talking about her years at the tower.

Marty said: "Randy, can you go up to the front counter and ask for a sheet of paper?"

I said: "Sure." As I approached the counter, I thought that he probably wants to write something down about the CCC camps.

When I returned to the table and sat down, he handed me a pen and said: "I want you to write down word for word what Helen told you about her years in the tower."

I wrote a page and a half. Marty remarked: "Don't you see! Helen wants someone to tell her story. I bet if you ask her this evening if she would like her story told, she would say yes."

I said: " But why me?"

Marty replied: "Because you know her very well."

Now it was time to go to the Grafton Inn. As we got there, the people were gathering. I gazed through the doorway and saw my mother approaching with Helen and her daughter, Connie. I went up to Helen and gave her a big hug.

3

Randy Kneer

I asked: "Helen, would you like me to write a story about you?"

She replied: "I would love that very much but it is going to be a big project."

I replied: "It would be a great honor for me."

The following week, I started my first interview with Helen at her house. I continued my interviews and research for almost two years. For me, it was like going back in time for the research required reviewing important events that were happening throughout the country. I became so immersed in the details that all I could do was write. I could actually envision myself being there with Helen in the tower. It was an awesome feeling.

Also at this time, I was facing a difficult challenge in my own life. Writing Helen's story was truly a blessing for it helped to keep my mind focused on positive things. I knew that this story was very important and it had to be told. Once it was finished, I had tremendous feelings of joy for I knew that many people were going to love reading her story. Helen is such an amazing woman. If you ever get the chance to meet her in person, then you'll know what I mean. She's one great lady.

Acknowledgements

I want to thank the following people:

Helen Ellett and her family for the wonderful times, the many stories, and the great information.

Diane Seaver, a wonderful friend who helped me edit and type this story. She is the Lord's blessing.

Marty Podskoch for giving me a chance to become an author. He is a true friend. I will always cherish him.

Helen Ellett's great-great granddaughter-in-law, Lindsay Baker, for designing the front and back covers for the book.

Bill Starr, Rev. William O'Dell of the Grafton Baptist Church, Harold Goyer, Paul Farhart, and Herb Hasbrouck. Each has been an inspiration to me and a great friend.

Ed and Sandy Slattery, terrific friends who gave me awesome information on the Berlin Devastation.

David Hayden for editing.

My family and friends for moving me forward with this story. I'm so grateful for their love and patience with me.

Finally, my faith in God and in his son, Jesus Christ, has inspired and sustained me throughout.

On March 27, 2011 David Hayden, Randy Kneer, Diane Seaver, Helen Ellett, and Marty Podskoch gathered at Helen's home in Grafton for dinner.

I Remember When:
The Untold Story of Helen Ellett

I, Helen Ellett, was born on February 16, 1914 in Troy, New York in the middle of a snowstorm. As I grew up, the times were hard throughout the whole country. It was the era of the horse and buggy. I can still picture the trolley cars and the horse-drawn buggies clanging and clattering through the streets. A few cars were starting to appear from Henry Ford's assembly line. Horses have always played an important role in my life. I've had a special love for them ever since I was a young child. I remember the times when the Freihofer's wagon would pull up to our house. I always got a chance to pet the horses. That was a great treat for me.

4 generations Connie Alderman, Freda Babcock, Helen Ellett and Linda.

Also, I lived right across the street from the firehouse. Anytime the bell would sound at the fire station, I would run to the window. I really enjoyed watching the doors swing open and seeing the horses harnessed and ready to go. The driver on the fire engine would slap the reins and off they'd go.

Oh, the times were definitely different back then. People were always helping one another in times of need. If someone was hurting, then we were all hurting. We would all pitch in to be there for one another. Families stuck together. No matter what happened, we never gave up on those who were our own. We worked long, hard days. No one ever really complained because we were just so grateful to have a job.

We never had to worry about keeping our doors locked. Friends and neighbors trusted one another. Everyone was courteous

We had lots of fun together, too. Every day was a new adventure. We lived in Troy for quite a while. Then, we moved to Grafton when I was about six or seven years old. It was around 1921 and we lived with my grandfather. His house was right across the street from the Dunham House with the stone wall.

My Grandfather

My grandfather was a wonderful man. His name was Fernando Babcock. Grandpa was considered to be a jack-of-all-trades. He could fix anything. Everyone in the village called him 'Nan.' If someone needed something to be fixed or built, people would say: "Go and see Nan. He will take care of you." My grandpa was also a carpenter. He and my father built many of these houses around here and those down the mountain. They did it all for a dollar a day! And back then, you put in a long day's work.

As I was growing up, Grandpa taught me many things. He was the best teacher I ever had. Grandpa was the one who taught me how to shoot a gun. We would set some old cans on the fence in back of the house. Then, he taught me how to aim. In no time at all, I was able to hit each one without missing a single can. And that's how I became good with a gun.

Grandpa also taught me all about gun safety. His most important lesson was making sure that the safety was always on when carrying a loaded gun. "If it wasn't," Grandpa would say, "then accidents could occur."

Another thing Grandpa taught me was how to catch trout. He and my dad would take me fishing in the nearby streams. One of the best places for good fishing was the Little Hoosick River. Wow! There was always plenty of action there, and really big fish, too. Also, we fished all the streams this side of the county and we hardly ever got skunked because there were always plenty of fish in the streams.

Grandpa also taught me how to deal with a skunk. Yes. A skunk! You see, my mother had a henhouse and once in a while, a hen would die. Well, they would throw the dead hen outside of the henhouse. So this one time, Grandpa wanted to show me how the skunk would come in and take the dead hen and run off with it. When the skunk came around, we followed it way past the house. It went over the embankment and down to a level spot where there was a hole in the ground and there was the skunk's back end sticking out of the hole. My grandpa said that a skunk can not spray unless it is looking at you. When a skunk sprays, it flips its tail toward you. Grandpa even went over and touched the skunk without being sprayed. He said that you could do whatever you wanted to it as long as you weren't in front of it. You know, he was right! That skunk didn't even bother us.

Helen's grandfather Fernando Babcock, a master carpenter, made Helen a dollhouse. Her Persian cat, Tabby, would often invite herself to dinner as Helen's special guest.

I sure do miss my grandfather. He was a lot of fun. I loved my father a lot, too, and I miss him very much. He was always good to me even through the hard times.

My father and grandpa always worked together. They were always doing something. Their hands were never idle. My father use to paint designs on horse-drawn carriages. Everyone would come to him because he was so good at it.

My father loved musical instruments. He loved to play the banjo. My grandpa loved to make and play the fiddle. Boy, could they get everyone hopping. I can still hear the music playing. My daughter Connie learned to play the banjo, too. It was a great time!

My Younger Days

I can say that my younger days were really something. I was never bored and always had something to do. I had many friends. I remember that I used to hang around with Carolyn Boomhower. We were an adventurous team back then, always exploring old barns and abandoned buildings. You never knew what you were going to find. It was very spooky too! But that's one of things that helped to make it real exciting.

I remember one old building we entered on Dunham Road. The windows were gone. The roof had holes in it. As we walked up the stairs to the top room, there was an old bed. The springs were all that was left of it. An old rocking chair sat in the corner near the window that didn't have any glass. The curtains were still hanging and were blowing in the wind. In the other corner of the room was an old dresser with a vase-type jar still sitting on the top of it. We were very curious to see what was in the jar. When we looked inside, we got quite the surprise. There were ashes in it. They were someone's bodily remains. It made us so scared that we ran out of the room, down the stairs and out of the house. But we didn't stop there. We continued running across the street and then down the street for we thought that the remains was a ghost and it was chasing us. Nothing actually happened, except that we were frightened for several days after.

I have to say that the experience didn't stop us from continuing to explore old places. Oftentimes, we would find old bottles buried in the dirt and other interesting treasures in old dump sites. We did other things, too, when we were older, like belonging to the Grafton Trail Riders. We would ride for hours. Carolyn and I did so many fun things together.

Yes, I guess you could say that I was a tomboy. I did many fun things. I did things that were out of the ordinary like playing baseball and doing a few mischievous pranks. I was not afraid to try a lot of different things just for the thrill of it.

The old railroad from Berlin through Petersburg brought me more special memories with my grandfather. We could hear the blowing of the whistles from the steam engines all the way up to Grafton. My grandpa always brought me down to the Petersburg Railroad Station to watch the steam train stop at the station. It was such a beautiful sight! The huge steam engine puffing up smoke and pulling up to the station. It would stop to let passengers off the train.

Mostly everyone getting off was greeted by some family member or a great friend. I will never forget seeing all the love and affection that people had for one another.

Then the whistle would blow again and the train would be off for the next town. They should of never abandoned that railroad and tore up the tracks. Maybe they could still be used today. It's a shame that all that history is gone. Yet there are still a few remnants of the old railroad bed, like a few railroad ties and coal that had fallen from the cars. Sometimes, if you look hard enough, you might find an old spike or two lying near a piece of the rail.

Only a few of the rail stations are still standing today. One is in the village of Berlin and the other, which is in Stephentown, is starting to fall apart. The town Historical Society should think about doing some restoration before the station totally disappears. As you travel south of Stephentown, you can find a few more stations. When you think about it, trains were a great way to travel from village to village.

My early childhood days definitely helped to form me into the type of person who could handle the long hours alone while I was a fire tower observer. I was an only child and we lived with my grandpa. My mother

Frank Babcock, Helen's father, and his German Shepherd, Duchess, are taking a little rest in the family hammock. Frank was thought to be a real animal lover.

ran a boarding house. She rented out three rooms in our house to people who would come up from New York City. It had gotten so popular that my mother got the neighbors involved in renting out their extra rooms. It was a full-time job and my mother was constantly busy. She did all the cooking and served the meals. That's how I actually met my husband, Chet. Mom had a telephone work gang renting the rooms and he was one of the men in 1928.

My father was a carpenter. He, too, worked long hours, so I had to learn how to keep myself busy. As I've already said, I spent a lot of time hanging out with my grandpa. He was the best grandparent than anyone could ever want. We were very special to each other, and I will always treasure those special memories. He taught me boy's things instead of girl things.

When I was about five years old, my grandpa bought me a bank. He filled it with nickels. I played with that bank for hours. Also, I was not into playing with dolls. Instead, I would spend lots of time playing with the toy horse and cart that my grandpa gave me. He showed me how to make a fence for my horse and a little barn. Other times, my grandpa would let me use a hammer and some nails. I would spend long periods of time just hammering nails into a piece of wood. It made me feel like I was a carpenter just like my dad and grandpa.

Grafton Hill riders.

School Years

I was not able to go to school until I was eight years old. It was not too good. I went to a one-room schoolhouse that had about 40 kids from kindergarten to eighth grade. The school that I used to go to is the post office building today. They have since refurbished it. The bell is still up in the old tower. It is right in the center of town. The room was small and it had an old potbelly stove in the middle to keep warm in the winter. We used paper and pencils to write. The teacher had a chalkboard. We had to bring our own lunch with us.

Everyone wanted to be chosen to fetch a pail of water from a neighbor near to the school. If you had to go to the bathroom, you needed to use the outhouse. We didn't have bathrooms like today. School never really closed in the winter due to bad weather. The teacher usually lived near the school so it was always open. Other times, she would go by horse and carriage.

I remember how hard it was to walk to school. It was so cold. I would hurry and try to get there as fast as I could. Sometimes I used my skis to get there. I was the first one in town to own a pair of skis. During recess, I would go skiing up in back of the Catholic Church. At that time, it was all open fields.

Even though I was 8 years old, I had to start in kindergarten. Oftentimes the teacher was busy with the older kids. She didn't have time for the younger students. This made learning very hard because I just couldn't get interested in what I was supposed to do. We weren't allowed to walk around or cause any noise, so we had to find some way to keep busy.

I really disliked math. I found it very frustrating. My interest in school did not improve when I finally got to high school. I always felt that I was behind all of the other kids. I left high school at the end of my second year.

Not doing well in school didn't bother me because there was always something for me to do. When I got home from school, I had a few chores like feeding the chickens. Grandpa always helped to keep me busy and he made me feel that the work I was doing was real important.

In the evening, I liked to go into his section of the house. It was toasty warm and I would hear him and father talk about the news and scandals that were happening in town. There was a little saying: "Little pitchers have big ears." I still remember a lot of the gossip.

He showed me how to use my time wisely. He was forever making furniture out of small scraps of wood. Once, he made a cabinet out of old cheese boxes. The markings on the bottom of the boxes can still be read today.

Another time, he built the steeple on the Baptist Church in Grafton. The steeple was hit by lightning during a bad storm. The wind just about blew the steeple apart and the church almost burnt to the ground. So, Grandpa had to rebuild the steeple. We had some very violent storms back then. When the lightning and thunder came across the mountain, we hoped it would be over real quick.

I can remember one summer in 1925 when there was a big fire at the Scriven Shirt Factory. They made all types of shirts and shirt collars. Many of the townspeople were employed there. At the time of the fire, the factory was actually closed. The owner had opened a small grocery store in one part of the building. One afternoon, a fire broke out in another part of the building. Everyone gathered around to watch the fire. There wasn't anything that anybody could do. That same day, two other Scriven houses caught on fire. One was totally destroyed and the other one had some damage. People came from the city to see the destruction. A friend and I went around with tin cans and asked these people if they wanted to make a donation to the church.

I really enjoy the fall. I've always looked forward to that time of year. The colors of the maple trees are so beautiful. But when it is over, it is over! The leaves would peak and it seemed like in a few days, the wind would come through and all the leaves would be on the ground. When winter arrived, you knew it. It was cold. It was not uncommon to have the temperature drop to forty below zero. Sometimes it would stay cold for weeks. Our homes were not insulated like they are today. You had to have plenty of wood stocked up to stay warm or you used coal. I can still see the horses huffing steam from their mouths. It was so cold that every time you would breathe, your nose would stick shut. Cut your breathing right off. The trees would often snap off from all the heavy snow and ice. Many times, we'd get snow that was feet deep, not inches. Skiing was great. It was a lot of fun. I loved the winter even though it was cold and it went by fast. When the snow was gone, it was gone. The next thing you knew, the flowers were starting to pop up from the ground.

Then it was time for planting our garden for food. Whatever it took to survive, we did it all. We were never bored and always managed to get through the worst of times. We stuck together. I had a wonderful family.

I had a great mother, father, and grandfather. And we had great family gatherings. I loved them very much and miss them dearly. That's how I was brought up and learned how to survive.

Today, society is much different from the time I grew up. Kids seem to be spoiled. They are given everything. I had to learn to survive the hard way, and it was pretty hard. We had to put our resources together in order to survive. I fear that another Great Depression is coming because people don't know how to pull together or live without having everything they want. It will be much worse than back in the 1920's and 1930's. I can see it coming and it won't be long. Everything is way out of hand especially food prices, gas prices, insurance, and the costs of living. I have never seen anything like it in all my years. It's a shame.

I still think back to the old days when I was a young girl seeing the old trolleys, horses, and buggies, the Freihofer's wagon dropping off goods to the local restaurants and stores, the milkman delivering milk on the back steps of our home, the old trains running through Troy, and the fireman putting out fires.

I remember my father walking to work at Gurley's where they made thermometers and other things. I remember my father telling me that he was only late for work one day and it was because I was born. It was in the middle of a huge snowstorm. When he arrived at work late, he told them that he had a beautiful baby girl. They were very excited for him.

I will never forget Mom and Dad. They were wonderful parents and they worked very hard all of their lives. I am so proud of them. And to think, they never held me back from experiencing and exploring all that life had to offer. It all taught me how to survive.

Grafton

Living in the old town of Grafton was something to be truly cherished. The quaintness of the town was the glue that held everything together. Today, most of the forest up here is second growth because the first growth was cut down for farming. The farmer had to clear the land of all the trees and big rocks to make way for the fields to be plowed. Stones were placed in such a way that it made a fence to keep the cattle and livestock in pastured areas. Farmlands were slowly appearing all over the place. There is still some first forest growth left. You can tell by seeing some of the large trees that are over 100 years old.

I remember the horses during the winter months having plows hooked up to them. They would plow the heavy snow on the main roads all the way up through to the Village of Grafton. The Baptist Church had a stand for the horses of people who came to church on Sundays and for special events. The Methodist Church had the same type of stand.

Many of the old stone fences are still here today. If you look hard enough through the woods, you can see them. As you travel towards Petersburg, you can see them alongside the road.

Then there was the Scriven Shirt Factory. It was a big place and many of the townspeople went to work there. It was quite the friendly place because everyone knew each other. The factory did a lot of business. They made great shirts and other material items as well.

As I was growing up, I learned quite a bit more than most kids. My grandfather was a stickler about gun safety. He was forever teaching me more and more about it. His first words before every lesson were safety comes first. My grandfather always said that when you are carrying a loaded gun, you should always leave the safety on! When you were ready to shoot, then you take the safety off. There have been too many accidents with hunters in the past carrying a loaded gun in the woods with the safety off. They would stumble over a rock, trip, and fall. The gun would go off and seriously injure the hunter. Sometimes you heard stories that would be fatal. You can never be too careful. We were always doing a lot of target practicing. With time, I learned to shoot straighter and aim better.

My father never hunted. His passion was fishing. We would go trout fishing in all of the local streams. Grandpa was more into small game hunting. Once in a while, he would let me tag along. It was very exciting.

I loved getting up early on a cold November morning. We would have a great breakfast and then set out for the woods trying to find that perfect spot. Waiting quietly was the best. I had the feeling that down the road, I was going to be a hunter someday.

As I got older, the country was finally on the road to recovery after WWI. That was a terrible war. My grandfather and dad told me many lives were lost, but the country had to get involved. We had no choice.

As time went on, we started to see things change. Electricity finally came to Grafton. Automobiles were replacing the horse and buggy. That was definitely a better way to travel. Everything seemed to be going right for the country until 1929 when the stock market crashed. It was terrible. It was also the beginning of the Great Depression. I had an uncle that had investments in the stocks. He lost lots of money. The whole country was falling apart. People were losing their jobs in great numbers. Back then, Herbert Hoover was the leader for the country. It did not look good for him at all. It was a challenge we all had to face.

Mr. and Mrs. Frank Babcock

Also, it was a time when the country was suffering from another big problem, Prohibition. All alcoholic beverages were banned from the country. The country couldn't take a drink anymore. That was stupid. There's nothing like a good cold glass of beer. But it also developed into the time of the great gangsters like Al Capone, John Torrio, and Legs Diamond. Many people got in the way of these people and they were never seen again. It was pretty bad. But with time, things got straightened out. As for the Depression, many people were still loosing their jobs. Breadlines were forming all over the country. But we managed to pull all our resources together and survive all this.

My Wedding

One good thing happened during that time. I met the love of my life. His name was Chet Ellett. He was a lineman for the telephone company and he rented a room from my mother. We got to know each other because we had so much in common. He loved to hunt and fish. We went together for a while and then we got married in 1932. My maiden name was Babcock. Now it was to be Ellett. I was very much in love with him.

I'll never forget my wedding day. It was a bright, beautiful sunny day. The date was August 27th. 1932. Chet and I took our vows at the Babcock House with Reverend Samuel Spear officiating. We had just a few local people at the wedding.

My maid of honor was Marge Trumble who was known as Marge Snyder. Marge passed away a few years back. Marge was a good friend, and I'll never forget her. We did a lot together, too.

We all gathered after the ceremony and celebrated with a nice party. It was a fantastic day. The weather was perfect. We had decided to spend our honeymoon at Paradox Lake. Chet's brother and his wife drove us to a cottage on the shore of the lake. Chet and I didn't have a car back then. We knew that sooner or later, we'd have to buy one.

Paradox Lake is quite the place. The cottage we stayed in was perfect. It had everything we'd ever need. The view was breathtaking. The cottage had a deck on it where you could sit out at night. I can still hear the cry of the loons out on the water. What a sound! You could also hear the wolves and the coyotes howling in the woods. Owls were hooting in the nearby trees. The stars were beautiful and the moon was bright.

During the day, we took advantage of the lake and went fishing. Wow! Did we catch fish. We caught lake trout, bass, and pike.

Cooking was a little different. The cottage itself had a fireplace on the outside. We had to do all of our cooking there. We loved it.

Sometimes, we would walk to the nearest village called The Schroon Lake Village. The people were very pleasant. Overall, the week was perfect. It was a blessing to have weather like that. There's not too many weeks that are rain free. We were sad when the week had come to an end. It was such a romantic week.

Helen on Ginger

When we returned from our honeymoon, we knew that we had to get a place of our own. So we moved to Cohoes on Johnson Ave. We stayed there for only a short while and then moved to the lower end of Cohoes to Columbia Ave. It was on the corner of 5 James Street. We stayed there for a couple of years.

While we were living there, we had a beautiful baby girl. We named her Constance. We were proud parents. She was such a joy to have in our lives. Connie was born on October 10th, 1935. We knew that our home was too small and we would have to find another place to live. Also, we wanted a place that had a yard.

So, in 1936 we got our wish. We bought a place on Creek Road in Eagle Mills, NY. It was the perfect spot. The Postenkill Creek was right across from the house. The creek was a fisherman's paradise. Chet and I could practice our skills. Since the two of us loved to fish so much, we spent a lot of time there. We caught lots of nice trout. Some of the fish were quite large and you couldn't beat the beautiful scenery. The neighbors were nice, caring folks. This was truly the place we called home. We had lots of fun and great family gatherings. Everyone was always welcome to come in for a visit.

Eagle Mills was an old style village. It was beautiful. The old creamery, the general store, Hook's Blacksmith Shop, the firehouse, all were on the right side as you were heading towards Grafton. Today, that has all changed. Some of the old buildings are gone. The view is totally different.

I have to say that we were not hit too badly by the Great Depression. By then, we had a new president. His name was Franklin D. Roosevelt. He promised a change for the country. The New Deal was to put the country back to work and end all the poverty that everyone was facing.

Franklin was a great president. He took office in 1933. By the time Chet and I met, the country was starting to get back on its feet again. But there was a lot of trouble going on in Europe. This man named Adolph Hitler was bad news. What he was doing to people was awful. It was bad enough that we had to go through World War 1. I had the feeling that the country was headed for war.

Hitler was a bad man. He was named Chancellor of Germany in 1933. That's when the troubles seemed to have gotten worse. Hitler and his troops were invading other countries. It was like he was trying to take over the world. The United States was on alert. Some of the news on the radio was terrible. I felt so sorry for the poor people who this man was invading their country. Those countries did not deserve it. Many people were left homeless. Sometimes, the news was so bad that we had to just turn it off. To think, this country was making appliances and those countries were making bombs. But, we still had to get on with our lives.

Our General Store

We had a lot of great times on Creek Road. We stayed there for a few more years and then we moved. Chet found this beautiful place up on Route 2 in the Village of Quackenkill. It was across from Stuffel Street. Chet said that he always wanted to start a general store. He thought it would be fun to serve people. So we went together to take a look at the place. Chet fell in love with it right away. He said that it was the perfect spot.

So, we bought the residence. It was hard to say good-bye to the people on Creek Road. We had a lot of fun there. We left there in tears but we knew that we could always stop back and say hi to the people we had come to love so much.

So anyway, we bought the place in Quackenkill and built an apartment overtop the store. We turned the downstairs into the General Store. It was a perfect spot for the three of us. We even put a set of gas pumps out front. I remember pumping gas for the customers for $0.10 a gallon. I think it went as high as $0.12 a gallon. My daughter, Connie, attended school right across from the store. It was on the corner of Stuffel Street and Route 2. Today, it is the Hall residence.

The school was perfect for Connie. There was no cause for Connie to be late for classes. All she had to do was walk right across the street to get to school.

We had a good business at the store. We sold lots of goods, groceries, and a few handy things that people needed. The best of all was getting to know the many people who came into the store. They were a great bunch of folks and we all cared for each other very much.

Out behind the store, we had a barn, a stable, and a garage where I kept my first horse. Her name was Ginger. I got her in 1941. I kept plenty of feed and hay in the barn for her. On days when I was not busy at the store, I would be out riding. We'd take small trips on the many trails that surrounded the town. The Grafton Mountains were full of trails. Riding those trails gave me a sense of peace and inner joy. I could hear the birds, the sounds of the wind brushing up against the leaves.

The wildlife was incredible. The scenery at the top of the ledge was a sight to behold. Looking down over the valleys and the nearby mountains on a beautiful sunny day, could almost take your breath away. At times, it was difficult to leave but I knew that another day would soon arrive and I could return. I also knew that the store was waiting for me and the customers would be, too. We made a decent living there. It was hard work but we managed.

At this same time, the country was on high alert from what was going on in Europe. That man Adolph Hitler was worse than ever. And now, Japan was invading places, too. It wasn't good. This country was bracing for war. The troops were being called for stand by duty. The draft was starting up. I didn't like this at all. No one else did, either.

President Franklin D. Roosevelt tried to keep the country out of the war. He was doing a good job of it until we were attacked on December 7, 1941 at Pearl Harbor. We had a sneak attack by the Japanese. This was a big mistake. Many American lives were lost. Our Naval Forces were destroyed. Right after that, I feared we were going to be in a world war and, sure enough, we were.

It was a terrible day at the store when our country was attacked at Pearl Harbor. I can still see the people as they walked in. The sorrow and grief on their faces was unbearable to see. After a while, I, too, became silent and was filled with sadness. What could anyone say? It was a terrible time for everyone. I can still hear President Roosevelt's speech about it-- December 7th, 1941 a day of infamy.

Helen Ellet sweeping steps at Dickinson Hill cabin.

Before this time, President Roosevelt was doing a great job trying to get the country back on its feet. He even started the CCC Camps (Consersation Civilian), which helped our environment. Putting people back to work in these camps was the goal. People did things like build roads and bridges, clear bad timber in the forests. They did whatever it took to help the forest preserve. Today, a lot of the remnants of these camps are still standing. They were located all through this area, the Adirondacks, and the Catskills. Actually, they were all over the United States.

But then, things changed. The war was on. We all feared that this was going to last for a long while. And the draft was in full swing. Many people from this area were going off to war. The Watervliet Arsenal was going full force. As a result of this, Chet, got a job as a machinist and I got a job winding coils in an Airplane Defense Plant. We were both working very hard, harder than we ever thought possible. Trying to operate the General Store and work a full time job at the same time was tough.

We had another problem, too. With the war going on, it was hard to get supplies. Rationing had begun. Even gasoline was being rationed. We were only allowed so many gallons per week. If we had used up our rationof gas before the week was up, we were out of luck. We were limited in the amount of supplies we could buy because most of the goods were being sent off to the war. It was getting harder to run the store.

Fire Tower Observer

Charles Traver, the District Ranger, needed someone to be the fire observer on the Dickinson Hill Fire Tower. He stopped at the store and offered me the job. He told me about some of the duties. He explained that all of the wardens issued permits to people who ask for them to burn brush. Later, I would be told who was issued the permits. This was important because when I saw smoke in a certain area, I needed to check to see if the

The 60' high Dickinson Hill fire tower in Grafton with Helen looking out the cab window.

area had permission to have a fire. If the area had a permit, then it was OK. I didn't need to report it. But, if the smoke was in an area that a permit was not given, then I needed to report it right away.

One important thing that I always needed to remember was that all fires start small. And if the smoke was in the wrong area, then it could get very big in a matter of time.

One requirement for the job was to carry a pistol. I had to carry one just in case of danger. I was not worried about it because my grandfather had already taught me about guns and I had been shooting for a long time.

Also, I had to get fitted for a fire observer uniform. On that day, the man asked me if I wanted the zipper in the front or on the side?

I said: "On the side. What would I do with it in the front?" We all laughed. Oh, how proud I was at the thought of wearing such an important uniform. I loved it.

Another part of the job was to spot aircraft. Since the country was at war, it would be my job to report any aircraft that passed the tower.

As the winter came along, I started telling many of my friends about the new job I was going to start in the spring. They were excited for me, but they also had a few concerns. The job would start in April and last until about the end of October or early November. It was for seven days a week and the hours were from 8am to about 5pm. I really didn't care too much about that. I was paid $100.00 a month. One of my friends said that I was one of the first female fire wardens in the state. That idea made me more excited than ever. I knew that I would love that kind of responsibility.

Yet, both Chet and I were concerned about the General Store. We knew that we'd be very busy with our jobs. Also, it was getting harder to get supplies for the store. We couldn't help think about the possibility of having to sell the store. It really weighed heavily upon our minds.

On the morning of April 10, 1943, I rose up out of bed with such an excitement for the day. I was like an old chatterbox, talking nonstop about my new job at the tower. Then, it was time to get ready for work. As Chet was getting dressed for his job at the Watervliet Arsenal, I couldn't wait to put on my new fire observer uniform. I was proud wear it.

Before I knew it, it was time to saddle up Ginger. It was 8 miles one way to the fire tower. I didn't mind it one bit. The thought of riding my horse to work was actually a dream come true.

I'll never forget that day. It was a beautiful, bright, sunny morning. District Ranger Charles Traver said that he would meet me at the tower to show me the ropes. I remember visiting the tower as a child, but I never thought that someday I would be working there. Ever after I would often think how I was the luckiest person in the whole world.

Having Ginger was also a great blessing for she was very dependable. She was patient and had a wonderful temperament. I had another horse, too. His name was Rusty but he was not my Ginger. Ginger had to stay at the little stable all day, practically standing still until I was done for the day. Rusty wouldn't of handled that very well because he liked to be on the move and run fast.

Ginger on the other hand, liked to take her time and that was just fine with me. I really enjoyed a nice slow ride along the trails. It allowed me time to look at everything on the way; the trees, wild flowers and ferns, and the birds. Parts of the trail were a little tricky. Some areas were hilly and other parts were rocky, so it was important that we took our time.

As we arrived at the tower site, everything I needed was right there. The huge 60-foot tower was right in front of me and it stood very tall. As I looked up towards the top of the tower, I was taken in by what seemed like an endless flight of stairs to the cab. "Wow" I said to myself. "This is a big one."

Right across from the tower was the observer's cabin. It had a front porch and a perfect spot to plant my flower garden. Along the right side of the tower was a barn-style stable where I kept my horse. This place was perfect.

I was there for only a few minutes when I heard someone walking up the trail. It was Charles. "Hello Helen. I see you made it. Welcome to your first day on the job."

"Hi Charles. It's great to be here. This is quite the place."

"Oh, you're going to love it," he said.

I got off Ginger and put her in the stable. Charles told me to follow him. He wanted to take me up to the cab on the tower. As we were climbing the stairs, I was amazed at the view. I was also becoming very shaky the higher up we went. I told myself not to look down. I continued to focus on counting the stairs. There were 80 in all.

When we reached the top, Charles unlocked the trap door to the cab. As we climbed in, I couldn't help but think how different it was than what I had expected. The view was fantastic. The sky was perfectly clear. To the north, you could see the Adirondack High Peaks. I thought that I could actually see Mount Marcy, the highest peak. To the south, I could see the

Catskill High Peaks. On that same ridge, I could see the Number 7 Hill Fire Tower in West Stephentown. To the east, I could see the Taconic and the Berkshire mountains. When I faced the northeast, I could see the Bennington and Vermont mountains. To the west were the Kayaderosseras Range, where the Spruce Mountain Fire Tower was, and the Western Adirondacks.

The windows were a true blessing because they could swing open. All I had to do was unlatch the lock and within seconds there was beautiful fresh air. In the center of the cab was a table that had a topographical map of the area. The table also had an alidade to measure the location of the fire and a nice comfortable chair to go with it. On the wall hung a pair of binoculars and a telephone. We used the binoculars to look out in the distance.

Then Charles said: "Suppose you were looking out towards the Catskills Mountains and you spotted some smoke? You would use the alidade to measure exactly where the fire was located and at what degree. Next, you would need to check to see if the fire was a legal burn or not. If it was legal, then everything was ok. But if it wasn't, then you needed to report it right away."

Observer Helen Ellett uses the brass alidade to sight in on a distant smoke. She then used the alidade and map table to pinpoint the location of the fire.

Learning to use the alidade was very easy because Charles was such a good teacher. He went on to explain that the local wardens would have the reports of all the people who were given permits to have a burn. Every day, the fire wardens and the rangers would be reporting to me the names of these people and places where I could expect to see smoke. Also, they would be giving me details about the type of burn. Charles told me that I needed to check every small column of smoke because all fires start small and could get quickly out of control.

Finally, he told me that I would be looking out for airplanes. Since we were in World War II, I needed to be on the lookout for suspicious airplanes in the area because some of them could be enemy spy planes. Charles showed me a special number located on the wall. I needed to report suspicious planes to the Aircraft Filter Center right away.

Then, we had to climb down all those stairs. Going down was much easier than going up. Within a few minutes we were at the base of the tower and heading towards the cabin. This, too, was such a perfect place. It was like a mini home. It had a table and some chairs, a woodstove for heat and later, I had a gas stove to cook on and some utensils, too. There was a little sitting room and a bedroom. The place was more than enough for me as I would be spending most of my time in the tower.

Chet really helped me with this part of the job. He told me that he would come and stay with me if the time came when I would have to stay there all the time. Chet really put my mind at ease. Overall, Charles said the job was not too bad. The only tough times were the dry seasons, which were the months of April, May, and the fall season. The summer months could be tricky depending upon the amount of rain. Charles felt that this job was perfect for me and I had to agree. I knew that I would love it!

I got really excited when Charles asked me if I was ready to get to work and had I packed a lunch? I told him that I sure did. I had even brought my thermos full of coffee. So we climbed back up the stairs, all the way to the cab of the tower. We were there for the rest of the day watching for smoke. Charles told me that tomorrow I would be there all by myself. He felt that I had everything under control and would be just fine. As we climbed down at the end of the day, Charles wished me well. He told me that I could call him if I had any questions. I was never to hesitate.

I had some great help in those days. Sherman Barnhart was a warden. He was the owner of Barnhart's General Store in the center of Grafton. Also, Ranger Bob Hitchcock, over in West Sand Lake, was great at his job, too. Ranger Willis Gootermote from Stephentown and all of the neighboring fire towers helped me, too. There was the Cornell Hill Fire Tower towards the north in the Saratoga Lake area. It was about 14 miles away. The Colfax Fire Tower in Washington County was about 15 miles away. The Spruce Mountain Fire Tower in the northwest of Saratoga County was about 25 miles away and the Number 7 Hill Fire Tower to the south was about 10 miles away. Finally, the Prospect Mountain Fire Tower was about 30 miles away in Warren County.

When the day had ended, I went to the stable and got Ginger ready to head home. As we rode along the trail, I got very excited thinking about the day. I knew that tomorrow would be a new challenge and I was ready to take it on.

No sooner had I gotten Ginger all settled for the night, it was time to get supper started. Chet would be home in no time and I wanted to make something special to celebrate this great day. I couldn't wait to tell him all about my day as the new fire observer at the Dickinson Hill Tower.

I remember looking at the clock. It was after 6pm. I quickly got everything going. Soon, we were ready to eat. As we sat down, Chet asked how my first day was on my new job? I told him to tell about his day first because I knew I'd be talking for a long time. Chet explained that he had a rough day. The war was putting some real demands on the arsenal and he might have to put in some overtime. The extra money would come in handy.

Then it was my turn to share. I told him how nervous I was at first and that my legs got shaky as I went up all those stairs. But once I got to the top, the rest of it was a piece of cake. I told him all about the breathtaking scenery and how the views were fantastic. It was fun trying to pinpoint certain places using the map table and the alidade. I even had a list of all the people who were given a permit to burn for the day. We didn't see any smoke but I knew that I'd have plenty of opportunity to see some in the days to come.

Chet was impressed to know that I'd receive a new list of issued permits every day. He was also pleased to know the names of the people that I'd be working with. They were a great bunch of reliable men and that gave Chet some peace of mind. The job had a lot of responsibility to it and he knew that I was very serious about making sure that I did my part well. Chet was such a kind man. I told him that starting that next day I'd be all by myself.

He was not too keen on me staying the night there by myself. He assured me that when that happened he and Connie would join me for the night. We also talked about the dangers of being in the tower during a storm. Chet was very interested in knowing the plan. I explained to him how Charles told me that when a thunderstorm was approaching, I was to get out of the tower. Towers are a very dangerous place to be during a storm. They attract lightning so I needed to seek a safe shelter as soon as possible. If lightning actually hit the tower while I was in it, I might not live to tell about it.

Chet was surprised to learn that I would be watching out for enemy spy planes. I told him that was an added benefit and it made the job more exciting than ever.

Then our conversation turned towards our store. The war rationing was making it harder and harder to get supplies and both Chet and I were now working full time. We discussed the possibility of maybe selling the store. We decided to give it some more time before we came to a final conclusion.

After dinner, we turned on the radio to listen to the news. It was all about the war. The country was having a tough time. Some progress was being made but many men were losing their lives. Before we knew it, the time was 8:15pm. Connie needed to get to bed and I needed to get my things ready for the next day. We turned in about 9:30. I had a little trouble getting to sleep because I couldn't stop thinking about my day.

The next morning I flew out of bed early to get breakfast going. Then I got Connie and Chet up. We all got dressed and ate. I watched Connie go across the street to the school and Chet drove off to work. I packed my own lunch and got my thermos full of coffee. As I went out to the barn, I started to get a little nervous thinking about the day. But I knew I could do it. I saddled up Ginger and off we went. I told her: "Come girl. Let's get to work."

It was a beautiful day and in no time at all, we were at the tower. I put Ginger into the stable and got her some water from a nearby creek. I didn't have to worry about getting her hay. There was plenty of it already in the barn. I didn't have to worry about water for myself because on the right side of the observer's cabin was a water catcher. Every time it would rain, the water would be collected off the roof and run into a pipe that flowed into the cabin. The pipe was connected to a sink that had a faucet. It was great to use for washing the dishes and getting cleaned up, but I would never drink water from there. Instead, I got my drinking water from an open well that was nearby. It was safer.

The climb up the stairs to the tower wasn't any easier than the day before. I kept telling myself not to look down and to keep my eyes on the trap door. I concentrated on taking just one step at a time. It was such a relief to have my body inside that cab. I couldn't help but think about all of the other observers who came before me, like Elsie, Charles, Glenford Simmons and, of course, William Klaus. I'm sure that their knees were shaking, too, the first time they went up that tower.

From what I understand, those people only lasted a few days on the job. They found it to be very boring and lonely. They couldn't stand being in the small cab for such long periods of time. But I knew that it would be different for me. I didn't mind being alone and there was always something to do. It was at that time that I decided to replace the chair with a wicker one that I had at home. I had Chet bring it up the next time he came to visit.

Once I got myself together, I called the local warden, Sherman Barnhart, to get the list of permits that were issued for the day. Sherman answered and said: "Hi Helen. Welcome aboard." As he read off the list of permits, I wrote them down. It was also important to write the number of each permit.

Then, it was time to get to work. It took a couple of hours before I saw my first puff of smoke. I quickly pinpointed it on the map and measured it with the alidade. Then I crosschecked it with the list of permits. It was a legal burn. I still had to keep and eye on it just in case the fire got out of hand. It took a few hours for the smoke to stop. The rest of the day went on about the same way except that the phone kept ringing. It was everyone from the neighboring fire towers welcoming me aboard. They all told me that I would love the job. Some days would be more interesting than others, but overall I would love it. I did take some time to just sit and enjoy the scenery. I had unlatched one of the windows and swung it open. A light, warm breeze came in.

Helen gazing out the fire tower cab window enjoying the beautiful fall colors of red, yellow, and orange in the surrounding forests and neighboring countryside

As those early days went on, I lost my fears and would run up the stairs.

That year, we had a semi-wet spring. I spotted quite a few fires. Most of them were legal burns. Several fires were not legal and I reported them right away. Then the warden would have to go out to the site and make sure that the fire was out. Most of the time, the person was only issued a warning if it was their first offense.

Town of Grafton Fire Department Founded

At this time, the Town of Grafton did not have its own fire department. The town had to rely upon the other fire departments, like the Eagle Mills Fire Department and the Petersburg Fire Department, to assist them with any fires. Also, Grafton was growing quickly. More and more homes were being built. As the spring of 1943 ended, so did the wet weather. The summer turned very hot and dry. It was one of the driest summers that Chet and I had seen in a long time. All of the fire towers in the state were put on high alert. Since very little rain had fallen, all permits were canceled. No one was allowed to burn. I had to stay there at night on weekends because we were on high alert. Chet stayed with me. He and Connie loved coming to the cabin. It was like camping out.

By the end of the summer, a little rain had fallen but it was not enough. There were many fires being reported across the state. This was not a good sign. I will never forget the morning of September 12, 1943. I was looking south. I saw smoke rising up. I pinpointed it on the map and then used the alidade to measure the distance. It was coming from the Old Road (Route 2) down from the Village of Grafton. I picked up the phone and called Sherman Barnhart, the fire warden, who owned and ran the General Store. When he answered the phone, I explained that there was an awful lot of smoke coming from the Old Road and it was getting bigger and bigger.

Sherman said: "I haven't got time right now Helen. I've got too many customers here and I can't leave. I'm sorry but I can't help you."

As I hung up the phone, I had to think of something. I decided to call Bob Hitchcock. He was over in West Sand Lake. He told me that he would be there as quick as he could. Then the phone rang. It was Ernie Wemple, the observer from the Number 7 Hill Fire Tower. He said: "Helen, you've got a lot of smoke coming from your area. From what I can pinpoint, it's coming from the Old Road."

I told him that I was having it investigated right away. He told me that he was going to contact the local fire wardens to get them out there. I told him that I had called all over, too. Then I thanked him and told him how much I appreciated all of his help. I left the cab of the tower and went down the stairs as fast as I could without missing any steps. I remember running down the trail to the nearby lumber mill. It was owned by William Henry

O'Dell. Young William O'Dell was there, too. (He is now the Reverend of the Baptist Church in Grafton.)

I told Henry about the fire. He got all of the workers from the mill together. They grabbed shovels and whatever else they thought would help and drove towards the smoke. When they arrived at the scene, everyone could not believe what they were seeing. The whole area was a total loss. The barn had already burned to the ground. The heavy wind did not help the situation. By the time the fire wardens got there, nothing was left.

Later, we found out that it was a resident who had carelessly started the fire. The person had gone outside to light some papers on fire, then went back into the house and didn't pay any attention to the fire. The stiff, blowing wind spread the flames to some nearby lumber from a neighbor that was leaning against the barn. It caught the barn on fire and then it spread to the house. The intense winds fanned the flames which made everything burn so quickly.

The whole Town of Grafton was upset by this fire. They had several discussions about it and decided that it was time to form their own fire department. Many people said that it should of happened a long time ago. So, in the spring of 1944, Granville Hicks, Everett Wager, Chet Ellett, and some other local people got together to form the Grafton Fire Department. The first Chief was Henry Jack. This was such an important move for the area because it took a lot of pressure off the other local fire departments, although they were still willing to help out if the need arose.

As time went on, I continued to have my job at the tower and Chet had his at the Arsenal. We decided to close our General Store as it was getting harder and harder to run the store. Also, we decided to put our home up for sale and move into my grandfather's home which was up in Grafton center. It was known as the Babcock House. Once we moved in with my father, mother and grandpa, my horseback riding to and from the tower was cut by four miles. But for Chet, it meant that he had to drive four more miles to work. Overall, it worked out just fine. Connie was able to go to the school just up the road. It was the same one that I had gone to as a child. Connie really enjoyed it because it was a change from the other school and at the end of the school day, she only had a short walk home.

I just loved living with my parents. Grandpa loved it too. It took a little while for Chet to get used to it, but he finally did. We were very fortunate to be able to have many dinners together. It was always like a family reunion.

After dinner, my father would go into the living room and turn on the radio to listen to the news about the war.

I'll never forget one particular broadcast. It was June 6, 1944. It was the invasion of Normandy. D-Day as it was called. Our troops had landed on the beaches. We listened to the announcer tell how many of our men had died just trying to get onto the beach. The amount of casualties seem so hard to believe. We all sat there in horror of what we were hearing. We were trying to be hopeful, but sometimes it was too hard to listen so my father would get up and shut the radio off. He would remind us that the American forces were doing the best that they could, but it would take time to win this battle. I knew that he was right. Our country was strong and this war had to come to a positive end. It made me proud to be an American and a fire tower observer.

Being the tower observer was not a simple job. It included many other duties. I had to keep up the grounds. I planted a flower garden and tried to keep the area clean. Sometimes, I needed to mow, pick up all the leaves, and clean up any debris from the fallen trees.

Soon after moving into the observer's cabin Helen designed her flower garden. The daffodils were the first to be planted for they signaled the beginning of a new year in the tower.

Painting the outside of the fire tower was a scary task. Painting the cab took some special help. My father and the rangers would always come to help out. To paint the roof of the cab, we had a big plank board that would extend through one window and out from the other side. One person would stand inside on one end for weight while the other person, my father, would stand outside the cab on the plank to paint. It sounds crazy but that's how it was done in those days. We had no other way to get out there to paint the roof. The men did wear some safety ropes just in case they fell. We all would give a sigh of relief when that job was finished. No one really looked forward to doing it. Every day and every season had its own adventures. It was never a boring job for me.

I can still remember many times when I saw smoke. A lot of the fires were started carelessly. Sometimes, it was lightning that sparked the fire but more times than not it was someone being careless.

District Ranger Charles Craver told me that if I saw a thunderstorm coming, I was to get out of the tower as quickly as possible. Well, one hot summer day I saw a huge thundercloud approaching from the west. I knew that this wasn't a good thing so I ran down the tower as fast as I could. As I got to the cabin, I looked back at the tower. I saw lightning strike. It ran down the wires and was grounded. Luckily, no damage was done. If I hadn't got out when I did, I wouldn't be here today.

Another time in 1944 I decided to take my other horse, Rusty, to work. On the way home, we came across a timber rattlesnake on the trail. It was shaking its tail and was all coiled up ready to strike at us. Rusty instinctively reared up. As I held onto the reins, I was able to get him off to the side. I was grateful that the snake never actually struck at us.

Seeing snakes around the cabin was not uncommon. Often, I would see the puffed adder snake (the hognose snake). Many people thought they were poisonous but they aren't. When this snake gets scared, it will rise up and form a hood like a cobra and try to scare you. A lot of times, they will try to play dead. I was never worried.

That night, when I told Chet what had happened, he said: "Helen, you can never be too careful because you don't know what you're going to see. I know that there are black bear in the area."

I have to say that I never saw a bear. There were several deer that would come around the tower but never a bear. I had heard that other people in the surrounding area saw a bear or two, but I never did.

On some of my days off, I loved to go horseback riding on local trails.

Chet would come along, too. We had kept our horses in my grandfather's stable. I love horses and I still do today. I was at the tower one day and the phone rang. It was my Uncle Walter Weigner.

He said: "Helen, I've got a horse for you. If you don't like him, you can give him back to me." I couldn't believe my ears. He told me that he was going to put him in the stable. The day seemed to drag. It was all that I thought about for the rest of the day. When I got home, there he was. This beautiful Appaloosa was standing in the barn.

As I stood there looking at him, I remembered seeing him before. For a number of years, I went to a place called Mae Fonda's in Cohoes to hang out with other riders. One day, I was mentioning a horse that I had been thinking about buying. It was an Appaloosa. But when I went to check his feet, the horse stomped.

I said: He's not for me."

Mae said: " You don't want that one. He is always bucking off his owner-rider."

Wouldn't you know! That was the horse Uncle Walter was offering me. But I didn't care. I had to ride him. I saddled him up and off we went. At first, he bucked a little but then he calmed right down. He turned out to be the best horse I had ever had. I named him Smokey. I loved taking him to work.

Helen rode her horse Smokey to the Dickinson Hill fire tower

One would think that the tower was a lonely place, but it wasn't. Often times I would get groups of visitors. Many of them were hikers. They wanted to know if the tower and the land it was sitting on was the highest point in Grafton? I had to tell them it wasn't. The highest point is off of the Snyder Road which is off of the South Road. I told them to follow Snyder Road to the end where there is a wooden observatory lookout tower. The tower is 1995 ft., which is the highest point. The reason it is not at the Dickinson Fire Tower is because the Dickinson tower is situated in a spot where we have the best view of the valley.

A lot of times, the hikers complained about a certain resident who had given them a hard time about going to visit the tower. The local rangers and neighbors tried to speak to this person, but they were unsuccessful. That resident was so stubborn. Often times, this person would actually measure the land that the tower was sitting on and claim it was private property. But it was not true. The Conservation Department had a lot of trouble with this person. It didn't make any sense to me that someone could be so rude. The only thing the hikers wanted to do was visit the tower and enjoy the view. I was always very happy to receive visitors. Chet would often drive up to the tower after work and visit with me. He always wanted to make sure that I was ok.

He was very handy, too. Chet knew how much I loved horses and so one day he put up a fence so I could feel more secure with my horse. Inside the corral we had a trough that had plenty of water in it. I also made sure there was plenty of hay. This was important to me because being at the tower was like being at my second home.

In the fall of the year, the view was spectacular. Looking down into the valley and seeing all the beautiful colors was a sight to behold. I never got tired of it. I always thought how lucky I was to have this job. Then, winter would set in and it was time to close up the cabin.

In 1945, changes were beginning to happen with our country. I remember listening to the radio with my family when the news came over the wire about the attack in the Pacific Ocean. Our country had taken over Iwo Jima from the Japanese. It was a great victory.

Helen used the tower telephone to call the local forest ranger or fire wardens when she saw a suspicious smoke.

1945

The winter seemed to go by very fast and before I knew it, I was back at the tower. It was April 10, 1945. A few days later, President Franklin D. Roosevelt passed away. It was a very sad day for our country. He had done so much for our country, like forming the Civilian Conservation Corps camps. We had a CCC Camp up here in Grafton. It was on the Taconic Road. Only the foundation of the camp remains today.

My job of looking for aircraft was far from over. I had to report all planes, even those that didn't look suspicious. I had to identify all aircraft. Also, it was a very dry spring and many of the burning permits were canceled. I remember that one day I had over 18 fires to report. All of them were illegal and they needed someone to check on them right away. Sometimes I had to stay up in the tower for over 12 hours. I couldn't leave until all the fires were out. Ground fires were especially bad when they got out of control. The rangers needed to get all the help they could find to help put out the fire. It was not uncommon to see the fire wardens and firefighters bring in power pumps and an Indian tank filled with water strapped to their backs. The tank was a hand-held pump to spray water over the fire. Other men used shovels to throw dirt onto the fire.

Helen riding her horse Smokey to the Dickinson Hill fire tower. She was accompanied by her dog Tippy.

A lot of times the fire would burn underground because of debris that had been buried. It would cause the fires to re-ignite. Sometimes ground fires would last for days. They wouldn't go out until we had a heavy soaking rain. Times were tough during a dry spell. I can remember making lots of sandwiches and coffee for the men as they battled the flames.

Keeping the area around the tower clean and presentable was also a part of my job. Since I loved flowers, I planted many perennials. If you go to the tower in the early spring, you can still see them. They are near the old foundation.

July of that year was interesting in another way. On July 26, Ranger Traver called the tower. He told me about the terrible murder of a woman at a local fire tower. I was stunned. Charles told me that I needed to carry my pistol wherever I went. I couldn't be too sure that I would be safe. I was really uptight about the thought of staying at the cabin by myself.

When Chet called during the afternoon, I told him all about it. He was great. Chet reassured me that everything would be all right and I shouldn't get too worried over it. He wanted me home as soon as my job was done for the day. Later on, during the police investigation we learned that all the clues pointed to a lover's quarrel between a woman, her husband, and a jealous boyfriend. It seems that there had been a horrible fight and everything went bad for that poor woman. I had a hard time getting past this one.

Then on August 6, 1945, the United States dropped the atomic bomb on Hiroshima, Japan. Three days later, a second bomb was dropped on Nagasaki. After this, Japan surrendered and the war was over.

Now it was time for the country to start rebuilding and the season was coming to an end. Over one hundred fires had been reported. This was always a sad time for me because I loved being in the tower so much. But Chet and I were not at a loss because there was always something for us to do. We both loved to hunt. I also loved knitting, sewing, and painting landscapes. Many times we went square-dancing down at the old barn off of Long Pond Road. It was owned by Mr. Sulton. My favorite dance was the polka.

After a while, Sam Solton opened up his big dance hall behind his store on Route 2 in the Village of Grafton. Everyone looked forward to dancing on Friday and Saturday nights. Just about all the town folks were there. Everyone had lots of fun even if they weren't into dancing. Some people went to just enjoy the music and chat with all their friends. I can still hear that old fiddle a humming.

Before I knew it Thanksgiving had arrived. There's nothing like eating a fresh turkey. Turkeys that are bought in a store taste nothing like a wild turkey. Then came the Christmas season. It was and still is a very special time for us. A lot of the neighbors in town had put out their manger scenes and Christmas decorations. Many houses were all decorated. The horse-drawn sleighs were fun to watch as they went up and down the streets filled with all kinds of packages.

1946

The spring of 1946 seemed to come quickly. This was my third year as a fire tower observer and I couldn't wait to get started. Overall, it was a normal year. We had several fires but we also had a lot of rain which helped to keep the fire danger at a low. I was able to take a few days off to go horseback riding with Chet and spend some good time with Connie. As much as she enjoyed being in the tower with me, we always tried to do other things with her. She was 11 years old at that time and she loved to ride horses just as much as Chet and I. So, we'd put her up into a saddle whenever we could. I am very grateful for her. Connie is very special. She had to put up with things that most children would never have to.

Connie, Helen's daughter, with her pinto, Chicka. She was an avid horsewoman who rode whenever time allowed.

The rest of the summer was about the same until one September day I got the scare of my life. I was up in the tower when all of a sudden the wind started to blow. It kept blowing harder and harder. The phone rang. It was Charles Traver.

He said: "Helen, you better get out the tower as fast as you can. A huge storm is coming up the coast. It's bringing strong gusty winds that could be too much for the tower."

I told Charles that I couldn't get out. I had already been trying to get out but I was trapped. The trap door would not open. And now I'm afraid the wind might blow me right off the steps. He told me to hang tight the best that I could. The wind continued to pick up speed. The windows were rattling so bad that I thought they were going to be blown out. I could actually feel the tower swaying. The interesting thing was that the storm was all wind. It didn't rain. There was nothing that I could do but wait it out.

After a long while there was a lull in the storm. I knew that this was my only chance to get out. If I was going to do something then I needed to do it right away. I tried opening the trap door one more time I and got it! As quickly as it opened, I was out of there. I flew down the stairs and ran into the cabin.

Later that fall was to become one of the saddest days of my life. My grandpa, Fernando L. Babcock, passed away on November 9, 1946. He was 90 years old. I never felt so down in my whole life. He was such a great man and he taught me just about everything I knew. It was like a part of me died with him. Grandpa was so good to Connie and Chet, too. We buried him on November 12 at the Grafton Cemetery. Almost the whole town came to his funeral.

Thanksgiving was a very tough day for everyone. My grandfather's empty chair left us silent at times but it also helped us to tell wonderful stories about how he had touched our lives. My dad really struggled with Grandpa's death. He not only lost his father, but he also lost his best friend. As for Chet and me, we filled our lives by doing more with Connie. She was 11 years old and already riding her own horse. We taught her how to saddle up her horse and get him ready for a ride. We rode everywhere together.

After the war was over District Ranger Charles Traver contacted Chet. He offered him a job with the Conservation Department. Accepting the job made him a fire warden. He didn't work around here. His job took him about 50 miles south into the Catskills. Chet would stay there during the week and come home on weekends and on his days off. It was hard on the family, but good jobs were scarce. Our family had been through a lot and we knew that this was just another challenge. My father was soon to get a job as the town Clerk of Grafton.

1947 & The Grafton Trail Riders

In the spring of 1947, I was back into the tower. You always knew that I was there because one of the first things I had to do was raise the flag. It was a sign that the fire observer was on duty. Many hikers would comment how proud it made them feel to see the American flag flying high above the cab.

That year, the Conservation Department had set many bog fires. They were trying to clean up a lot of the deadwood that would feed a wildfire. These bog fires would last for days at a time. I had to spend long nights in the tower to make sure that they didn't get out of control. I didn't have to worry about most of them because much of the area was very swampy. The part I enjoyed most was when nighttime came. The fires looked like tiny torches scattered across the mountainsides.

Grafton Trail Riders and the Cambridge Riding Club are riding on Main Street in the Grafton Fourth of July Parade in the 1950s. The man in the foreground is Don Boomhower.

Horseback riding still remained a very important part of our family time together. We loved riding and many of our neighbors did, too. Slowly, more and more of the townspeople owned horses and wanted to join us on the trails. In late November of 1947, Bob Stevens, Bob Leonard, and I had a long conversation about forming a riding club. They loved my idea and thought it would be a wonderful thing for Grafton. We set a date for early spring of 1948. I couldn't wait to call everyone that I knew who had a horse. When the time arrived, we held our first meeting at Vick and Millie Brimmer's residence on Stuffle Street. I was made president.

We called ourselves The Grafton Trail Riders. We soon learned that in order to be incorporated as an official club, The Trail Riders had to own its own property. Sherman Barnhart's father told the club that he owned a parcel of land which was about one quarter of a mile from the store. The club was free to use that land and they did. Later, Sherman agreed to sell the property so the club could be incorporated.

My mother, Freda Babcock, lent us the money to purchase the land. Everyone in the group agreed to work real hard to come up with the money to repay my mother. We sponsored lots of horse shows, rodeos, and even held a bingo night whenever we could. All this work actually helped to make the club grow. Many people loved to ride horses and wanted to have an active role in being a part of it. Our good friends, Carolyn and her husband Don Boomhower, joined the club, too. Don was a big help because he knew a lot of shortcuts through the backwoods. He could take us wherever we wanted to go.

Even Connie loved being in the club. She had her own horse named Tarzan. He was a beautiful, well-natured Pinto. Connie rode him whenever and wherever she could. I loved it when she would come to see me at the tower on her horse. I was so proud of her. Overall, the club had about 100 members at that time. The club is still in existence today and still uses that land, which is located on the Trail Rider's Way.

Becoming a Hunter

Another life changing time in my life was when Chet asked me if I wanted to go deer hunting with him. It was Thanksgiving morning. We quickly got dressed in our cool hunting clothes. Then we set off into the woods. We sat behind a big rock and waited quietly. All of a sudden we heard the sound of a deer nearby. As it got closer and closer, we both had our gun sights locked onto a big buck. Before I knew it, Chet had fired his gun and dropped the deer. It was an eight pointer.

I knew right then and there that if Chet could do that, so could I. I didn't hesitate to go out on my own. I was good with a gun and Chet was often busy with his job. I can remember times when the deer would come right up to me. If it was a big one, then I'd let him have it.

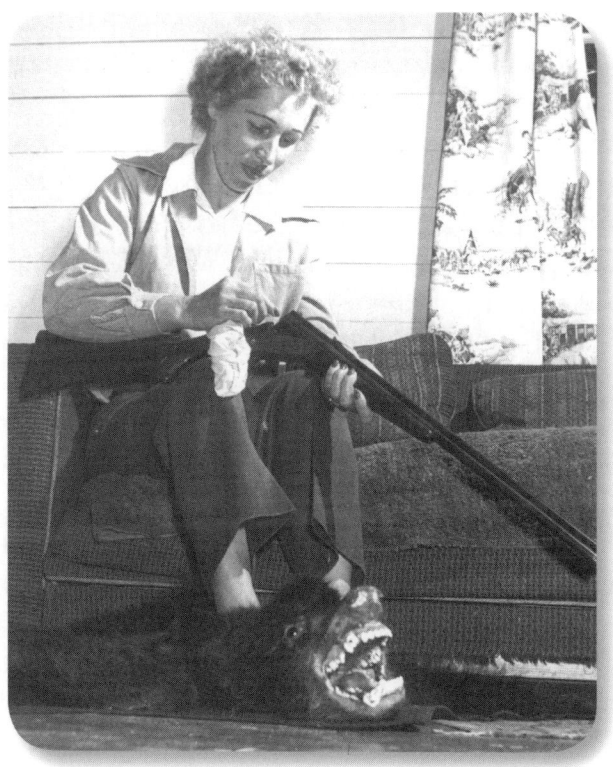

Helen cleaning her Remington rifle she used on her famous hunting escapades with Chet.

One of the best places to go hunting was right near the tower. I had a good view of the area and never failed to shoot at least one big buck and to see several spike horns. Gutting the deer and getting it ready to haul home was not an easy task, but it was worth it. The thought of those venison steaks made my mouth water. I loved hunting so much that I even wrote an article that was supposed to be put in the conservation magazine. It was called, "The Great Hunt."

Sadly enough, my story never made it into the magazine. But I didn't let that discourage me. As time went on, I started writing articles for the local newspaper. Many times people wrote to the newspaper and asked questions about my job. I had Chet bring me up a typewriter so I could respond to people when everything was pretty quiet in the tower. Other times, I wrote about different people who were doing interesting things in the area.

Believe it or not, I spent a lot of time answering phone calls for my mother. Mom was very well-known throughout the town. She was always doing things for other people. After a while, people began to rely upon her and it seemed like they constantly needed her help. She was a great woman. Both my mom and dad loved visiting with me in the tower. We had so many wonderful times up there together.

In the 1950's, The Grafton Trail Riders organization was in full swing. We had a big membership. We held many horse shows, rodeos, sponsored horseback riding trips, and entered some horseback riding competitions. Once, I won a trophy with my horse Smokey. We rode 40 miles in six hours, on October 1, 1950 in Ballston Spa. Also, we marched in many parades especially the Fourth of July Parade in Grafton. After the parade, we would put on an event called Frontier Day. Everyone would get all dressed up as cowboys and cowgirls and we held lots of different events. People would come from all over the state to be a part of this special event.

Then, in 1951, Frontier Town opened up in North Hudson. They didn't have the Northway at the time. Everyone had to go up Route 9. It was a nice road and many of us would travel all the way up there to see the rodeos. A lot of the cowboys were from the states of Wyoming, Texas, Montana, and Florida. Their shows were outstanding. They even had an old Number 44 locomotive with a few cars steaming up and down the tracks. They had men who represented the US Cavalry. They were all dressed up in blue and the lead horseman was holding an American flag. They had Indians who put on a show as they rode on their horses and a stagecoach being pulled by a team of horses.

Pets at the Tower

I remember a time when I had a pet raccoon at the tower. I got the raccoon when it was a baby. Chet and I knew this woman from a local tower who had a pregnant pet raccoon. I told her that when the mother had its babies to please give me a call at my tower. I wanted one so badly that I was even willing to pay for it. Some time later, I got the call. She told me that my raccoon was ready. All I had to do was come over and pick it up. So Chet and I did just that. She wouldn't hear of taking any money for it.

When I set my eyes on that baby raccoon, I immediately fell in love with him. He was so cute and cuddly. I called him Soggy. I had him for quite a long while at the tower. He would bed right down in the barn. Sometimes, he even stayed in the observer's cabin. The raccoon was so easy to tame. During the winter months, I would bring him home and he would stay in the stable. In the warmer weather, he was back in the tower with me. My German Shepherd dog, Tippy, loved to play with him. They would run all over the place and then lay down side by side to rest. They were so much fun to watch. Then, one day, the little guy disappeared, but he wasn't really little. Soggy was huge. I never saw him again. I had him for two years. Everyone loved him.

Helen's pet raccoon, Soggy, and her dog Tippy were playmates. It was not uncommon to see them romping around the grounds of the tower.

An Accident in Florida

Time passed. I met a woman who eventually became a good friend. Her name was Kay Beaupied. She loved horses just as much as I did. I got her to join The Grafton Trail Riders. Her husband Larry joined the club, too. Chet, Larry, Kay, and I made such a great foursome. We rode our horses all over the place. One day, she invited me down to her winter home in Florida. She told me that I would love it there. The winters are warmer than in the north and the weather is beautiful. I was really interested in seeing Florida but I knew I had to be back for the springtime.

Also, I was concerned about getting a job. I needed to earn some money to help support my visit while I was there. Kay told me not to worry about that for there was always plenty to do. In fact, there was a place that needed people to help train horses for harness racing.

I thought: "Harness racing. Doesn't that sound just grand!" Chet was not happy at first. He didn't like the idea of me being away, but with time, he gave in. So early in the winter of 1953, I set out for Florida. Kay and I both worked there. I fell in love with the job. I loved it so much that I actually considered quitting my job as fire observer at the tower and staying in Florida.

Then one morning, all that changed. I was at the track working with the horses. As I was going around the track, the horse stumbled and fell. Before I knew it, we were both on the ground. I was in a lot of pain. My ankle started to swell very quickly. Sure enough, it was badly broken. I was laid up for the rest of the winter. I knew right away that this was not the place for me. I couldn't wait to get home. Spring couldn't come quick enough. I longed to be back in the tower.

When that time did arrive, I had an unpleasant surprise. I arrived to work at the normal time but as I started to climb the stairs, my ankle began hurting real bad. I tried a few more steps but the pain was just too much. I had to call the Conservation Department and tell them what had happened. My dad was able to take over the job until I fully recovered. It took quite a few months for the ankle to completely mend. My dad was having a great time in the tower. He couldn't understand how I could have wanted to give up such an exciting job. He felt it was the best job that anyone could have ever wanted. I told him that he was right. How could I have ever thought of giving up the job I loved so much.

After Helen was relieved of her job, she and Chet decided to travel out west. They headed for Texas. Helen and Chet would often rent horses so they could get a better view of the hidden beauty tucked away in the countryside. Here, Helen is riding a horse named Mr. Chips overlooking a canyon in 1976.

Fired & More Writing & Travel

During that time I had to keep myself busy. I kept writing many articles for the local newspaper. It was a lot of fun to interview different people and write stories about them.

By the early spring of 1955, I was ready to get back into the tower. While waiting for that day to arrive, I received a call from the Conservation Department. They said: "Helen, there has been a change and you are no longer needed as a fire tower observer. It isn't that you're not good at your job. We love the work that you're doing, but it's really due to a political change." They promised to keep my name on the list just in case the job became available again.

This was a big blow to me. I couldn't believe that I had lost the job. I was devastated for a long time. Chet was great. He kept telling me that it was not over yet. They will need you again. It might take a little while but they will call you back for the job. I wished I was as positive as Chet. He got me to realize I was one lucky gal. I could have been killed on that harness track, but I wasn't. I needed to stop feeling sorry for myself and move on. I had so much to be grateful for. I had a wonderful husband and a daughter.

Connie had met a wonderful man named Larry Alderman. They were married that very same year. After the wedding, Chet came up with a great idea. He felt it was time for us to do a few things together. He always wanted to travel and felt this would be a perfect time to see the country. We got a travel trailer and drove it everywhere trying to visit as many states as possible.

One of my favorite states was Colorado. What a great place. I loved seeing the Grand Canyon and the Rocky Mountains. We even took time to do a little horseback riding through the mountains. When we would come to a brook or lake, we'd stop to do some fishing. There's nothing like fresh trout cooked on an open fire. Mount Rushmore in South Dakota is another site that everyone should see.

My favorite state in all of our travels was Texas. This was some state! Horses and cattle were everywhere. I never got tired of seeing them on the range. They made me long to be with my horses at home.

Back at the Tower in 1960

While we were gone, Chet and I became grandparents for the first time. Connie had a beautiful baby girl named Linda in 1957. We were so proud of her.

In the late winter of 1959, politics changed. I got a phone call from the Conservation Department. They wanted to hire me back for the job at the fire tower. I was honored by their offer and immediately told them: "Yes. I'll take the job."

By now things were a little different. I didn't have to ride my horse. I could actually drive to the tower. Yet sometimes, I couldn't resist taking Smokey to work. I had a lot of fun redecorating the cabin. I put up new curtains and cleaned the whole place up.

On my first day back, the phone was constantly ringing. Many of the neighboring fire observers were calling me to welcome me back on the job. They all said: "Helen, it's great to have you back. No one else has been able to fill your shoes." They made me feel so welcomed and appreciated. I knew that I was home again.

In 1960, Connie had another baby. They named him Bill. Chet and I were once again so proud to be grandparents.

As time went on, I was well-respected for the work that I was doing. Victor D. Schrader was the District Ranger. He was different from Ranger Traver. I was just grateful to be back on the job, raising the flag every morning and watching out for fires.

In 1961, Helen guided her fearless 4-year old granddaughter, Linda, all the way up to the cab of the 60' tall tower. There Linda would draw and color scenic pictures just like her grandmother.

Disaster in Berlin

I will never forget the fire that happened on July 25, 1962. The day had been very quiet. The fire danger was at a low and it was almost time to go home. All of a sudden, I heard a huge explosion. I could actually feel the ground below the tower shake and the glass in the windows rattled as if they were going to shatter. As I looked to the south, I could see a large plume of smoke rising up into the air. I checked the map and then used the alidade to pinpoint the area. Sure enough, it was located in the town of Berlin. I picked up the phone and called the rangers. I talked to Willis Goodermote who told me that he would get there as fast as he could.

Everyone I spoke to had the feeling that it was some type of disaster. I remember calling my dad. He said that he would get over there as fast as he could to investigate what had happened. I had opened the windows of the tower. I could hear sirens going off in the distance. Sirens were sounding from the nearby fire stations. I tried calling the different fire towers to see if anyone had found out what happened. It took time for the report to come through.

Finally, I got a call from the Number Seven Fire Tower. The observer told me that a propane tanker had rolled over at the bottom of Plank Road in Berlin. Several buildings and homes were on fire. Shortly after that, Chet called. He told me that people had died in the explosion and that the area was a total disaster. The devastation was hard to believe. I wanted to leave the tower and get right over there, but I knew that I couldn't. I had to stay on the job because that's where I was needed the most.

I watched the fire for a long time. I kept in constant contact with many of the other tower observers. We were trying to determine what was happening by the way the smoke would rise and fall. Later that evening, I heard that fire companies had been called in from all over. Several people had died and many more were taken to the hospital with severe burns. The news reporter went on to say that a tractor trailer tanker loaded with 7,000 gallons of liquid propane had overturned on one of the bad corners on Plank Road next to Berlin. Some people reported that it sounded like a bomb had exploded. They saw a huge ball of flames that had spread everywhere. It had leveled half of Berlin. Several people were screaming as they were running down the street totally on fire. Many of the buildings and homes were completely engulfed in flames. The 132-year-old First Baptist

Church was totally destroyed.

The next day, everyone was talking about what had happened. The stories of how loved ones were burnt to death made many people feel sick inside. Later, I was told the tanker was going the wrong way. It was not on the correct route. He should of never been on that particular road. The road was too steep and it had a few tough curves for a truck like that. Most people were left with trying to answer the question of how could something like that have happened in such a place as Berlin? After a while, Berlin needed to move forward. They started to develop plans on how to rebuild their town. Everybody did what they could to help.

I continued to stay on as the fire tower observer for only a few more years. My life began to have some big changes. My dad passed away on April 24, 1964. This was another great shock for me. My dad had always been by my side. Whenever I needed his help, he was there. I could always depend upon him. Chet took it really hard, too. We had done so many things with my parents. It was hard to believe that he was gone. He had many different jobs throughout his life. Dad was the town clerk for 36 years. He was even Deputy Sheriff for Rensselaer County and a fire observer for one year. I can't say enough about him. He will always hold a special place in my heart.

1965 brought a close to my time in the tower. I started working the season right on time but then my mother took ill. She was diagnosed with cancer. I quit my job to help take care of her. I knew that I would greatly miss it but, as grandfather would say: "Family comes first." I knew what I had to do. My mother passed away the following year. It was another very difficult time for me. The loss was hard to handle. Mom was so special in her own way and I was grateful for the time that I had with her.

Now I found myself without a job. I still had another 10 years before I could retire. A friend of mine told me of a job with the State Income Tax Department, but it turned out to be part-time. Then Evelyn Gifford told me about an opening at the State Office Building at the canal in Waterford. I worked there for a short time until another job became available at the DOT in Albany. I worked there until I was 55. I received a small retirement. At the time, Chet had already retired from the Arsenal which made our income easier.

Snowmobiling Fun and a New Club

Snowmobiling fun

At the time, I found the winter months to be very long. I needed some type of hobby to help fill my time. Larry, Connie's husband, was into snowmobiling. One day, he asked me if I wanted to go for a ride. I could sit behind him. It sounded like fun so I took him up on his offer. After one ride, I was hooked. I needed to have one of my own. Larry helped me to find one that was just right. It was a Snow Jet Road Runner. Boy, did I have fun with that thing. Later, I purchased a Yamaha.

I remember going on a lot of rides with Irv Mason and his wife Shirley. Irv was so much fun. He knew a lot of great trails to ride on.

Often I thought about all the fun The Grafton Trail Riders have and maybe we should start a snowmobile club. It didn't take me long before I was on the phone calling everyone I knew who had a snowmobile. I called Janet and John Smith, Ray Boomhower and many more. I asked them if they wanted to join the club. We had 25 people. We called ourselves "The Grafton Mountain Snowmobile Club." We rode all over the Adirondacks, across lakes and would stop to have some lunch along the way. We cooked hot dogs over an open fire and had plenty of coffee and hot chocolate.

With time, I got to know a friend from the Black River Raiders Snow Club. One day, he asked me if our club wanted to join him up at Big Moose Lake. He told me that everyone would have a great time because it was such an awesome place. We did have a great time. We rode across the Fulton Chain of Lakes, the Fourth, Sixth, Seventh, and Eighth lakes. Then, we went across Raquette Lake and rode all the way to Long Lake and back to Moose Lake.

One time, as we were riding down the road, this fellow wanted to race me. I said: "Ok," and quickly sped off. I knew that I was in the lead. But then I looked back to see where he was. The man was nowhere in sight, so I slowed down. I decided that I should go back and check on him. I found him. He had lost control of his snowmobile and scratched it up. "Boy, did he do a good job." His wife was furious.

I always looked forward to the great dinners and wonderful drinks after a day of riding. There's no place like the Big Moose Inn. Our club always looked forward to joining up with the Raiders. We would all manage to meet at the Big Moose Inn every winter. Every once in a while, I still enjoy taking a bus trip up there in the fall. You can't beat the beautiful colors, the wonderful scenery along the way, and best of all, an awesome meal at the Big Moose Inn.

Show Committee 1952

Saving My Tower

In 1972, I heard that the Dickinson Fire Tower was being decommissioned. It was easier to spot the fires from an airplane. I didn't like the idea too much. I felt that they were wrong. Planes could easily miss a fire, but the state wanted to hear nothing of it. They needed to save money. That was the beginning of the closing for many fire towers.

The thing that aggravated me the most was that the towers were actually being dismantled. Many people started questioning the process. What if the state ran out of money and couldn't afford planes any more? How would they keep an eye on the fires? But it didn't matter. The state went ahead with their plan. Soon, the land in which the Dickinson Fire Tower and the cabin rested was sold to the New York State Police. They wanted to put a radio repeater on the fire tower. Another great part of me died that day. I always hoped that someday, maybe, the Grafton State Park would purchase the property and make it a part of the state park.

Also in 1972, we moved into our new house. We built it on the Trail Riders Road, right next to the clubhouse. While it was being built, we stayed at the Granville Hick's house. It was a very interesting place. They had snakes living in the basement.

I really enjoyed their neighbors. They were Bob Wagar and his wife. They made the winter go by real fast. Before we knew it, we were living in our new home. I still live there today with Connie. I did sell my father's house after he died.

In 1975, I was able to retire from the State Department of Transportation. It was one of the best things that had happened to me in a long time. I didn't have any trouble keeping busy. I kept writing articles for the newspaper. Also, I spent a great deal of time with The Grafton Trail Rider's Club. We sponsored more horse shows, rodeos, and horseback riding trips. Chet and I even took time to go traveling again. We always had the trailer hitched up to the car especially on the weekends.

In 1985, Connie's husband passed away. It was another big shock for our family. Larry was a wonderful guy. Everybody loved him. Time passed and in 1993, the newly formed Friends of Grafton Lakes State Park started talking about restoring the tower. They were interested in seeing if the State Police would donate the land to the park. In this way, the tower could possibly be restored. There was a fellow named Ben Hill. He was one of

On July 14, 2010 Friends of Dickinson Hill fire tower visited the fire tower to celebrate news that the tower would be saved. Pictured L-R: Bill Starr, Grafton State Park Naturalist Liz Wagner, former observer Helen Ellett, Grafton State Park Manager Melissa Wagner, and Dick Gibb chairman of Dickinson Fire Tower Restoration Committee.

the founders of an ongoing effort to restore the Dickinson Tower. Ben was a great man to have on the job but he unfortunately passed away. The rest of the organization did not drop the ball. They picked up the pieces and continued the fight. Everyone was praying for some type of breakthrough with the State Police.

In 1995, my husband Chet died. That was the biggest blow to me. What would I do without Chet? He was my everything. I loved him so much and now he was gone. Connie and I began to really rely upon each other. We did everything together as we still do today.

In 2001, plans were well under way for the tower to be placed into the hands of the park. Everything was going smoothly until the attack on the World Trade Center in New York City on September 11th. All the plans for restoring the tower came to a screeching halt because of security defense reasons. I felt that the plans to restore the tower were finished. Many people told me not to give up hope. My dream would come true someday. I constantly prayed that God would intervene.

Sure enough, on July 9, 2010, I was informed by Randy Kneer that the time had come. My dream was about to become a reality. Randy, the Vice President of the Friends of Grafton Lakes, told me that he had heard from Bill Starr. Bill, the director of the Forest Fire Look Out Association and a former observer at Pillsbury Mountain Tower, had signed an agreement. It stated that the Dickinson Tower was now in the hands of the Grafton State Park and it was being scheduled to be restored. On July 15, 2010, Randy picked me up in his jeep and drove me to the tower. We were going to meet the officials from the state park. They wanted to take pictures of this historical moment.

I was so excited about being back at the tower. Words can't describe my inner feelings. I wanted to climb into the cab one more time but I knew that my legs would not let me go up all those stairs. If only they could restore my body like the old tower. I had to rest in the thought of knowing that my prayers were answered. That's all that really mattered. The tower was going to be restored and it would become a place for people to come and visit. Some of my family members had joined us at the tower. As the pictures were being taken, I could only smile at all the wonderful memories that this tower had given me as one of the first woman fire tower observers in the area.

Unpublished 'story'

It all started 10 years ago on Thanksgiving Day, after a big dinner. Chet took up his rifle for the second time that day and let it be known he was going out for a while, hoping to get a shot at a buck. Also, he convinced me I needed some fresh air and suggested I go along. Well, I like the woods, and thought some exercise might help to burn up a few extra calories which I could do without. So, away we went.

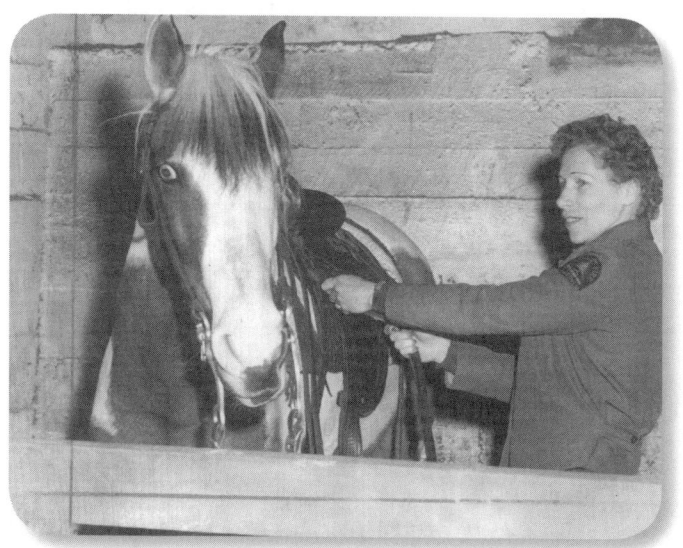

Helen saddling her horse Tarzan for a trip to Dickinson Hill fire tower. She is wearing her observer's uniform.

We drove up a narrow, muddy road. It had been raining earlier that day. We parked the car and hiked ¾ to 1 mile into the woods. I didn't take this thing too seriously as I didn't expect to see a deer. Chet picked a spot on a rock ledge. He leaned up against a birch tree, stating that this was a likely spot for a deer run. We each leaned against the tree, Chet looking in one direction while I looked another way. We looked and listened and listened and looked. I thought I heard an ever so slight movement in the direction of the brush at the foot of the ledge. I nudged Chet, putting my finger to my lips. "Shhhh!" Chet couldn't hear a thing. He shrugged his shoulders and turned looking the other way again. Chet moved from one foot to the other, blew his nose, coughed, and all this time I stood staring down at the ledge. I was strongly thinking of suggesting that we go home, as I was getting a little chilly.

Then without warning, a deer appeared up the ledge about 40 feet from us. I gently poked Chet who was looking the other way, and pointed to the deer, which by this time had scented us and stopped. Chet raised his rifle.

Not seeing any horns, he lowered his gun. As he did so, the deer tipped one ear forward and there was a horn, just about as long as those velvety ears.

I whispered: "It's a buck! Shoot!" Chet shot and the deer spun around and headed down the ledge.

I said: "You missed him." But Chet didn't see how he could have. We walked over to where the buck stood and discovered a splash of blood. Chet said: "Just because the deer takes off doesn't mean we didn't get him." I wasn't so sure. I was afraid we had seen the buck for the last time. We followed the blood signs and upturned dirt and leaves that were scattered by the buck's hooves. About 100 yards away laid one dead outstretched deer. Chet gutted it out and it bled real good. Then he somehow slipped the front and hind legs together and got the buck onto his back. I carried the gun. After many stops, we finally got it to the car. We felt pretty good about the whole thing and hurried home as fast as we could. We did make a few stops, of course, to show off the deer.

The next year as hunting season was about to open, I expressed a desire to get a gun and hunt, too. Chet was glad and on opening day he found me all dressed up like something from another planet with license and a 8 mm rifle in hand. It was pretty cold, so I put on snuggies, woolen socks, slacks, a woolen shirt, stadium boots, and to top it off a pair of olive drab navy overalls that belonged to my father. They were much too big for me. The legs were all bunched up around my legs and the bib went right up to my chin. Then I had put on a bright red hunting shirt with, of course, a red hunting cap. I was so bundled up that I could hardly walk.

Somehow, I managed to get to a good spot in the woods. I sat along a stone wall that had tall hardwood on one side and some scrub pine on the other. I stopped to tell Chet that I was going to hunt from there. He went up ahead toward the creek and then out of sight. I stood there propped against the tree. I needed a prop because of all the heavy clothes I had on. I stood perfectly quiet, straining my eyes and ears. I must of stood there like that for over an hour. Then out of the corner of my eye I saw some movement on the other side of the wall. I turned my eyes in my head as far as they would go. I saw a deer come quietly through that opening. But that wasn't all I saw. I saw another and another and another, big ones and little ones. It was actually the whole darn family.

"Oh why wasn't Chet here I thought." Five deer were there in all. I was so excited that I forgot to breathe. I picked out the buck, aimed, and fired. They all turned to look at me and I stood there looking at them. Then it

Chet Ellett, at tower in spring 1951

dawned on me that I was supposed to shoot the deer, not just look at it. I aimed and shot again. I shot too low. The bullet went under the deer, scattering the leaves and also the deer family, waving their white flags bye-bye. Chet came puffing up the hill. I excitedly told him about the deer family and pointed in the direction in which they had gone.

Well, that's all I saw for the rest of the day. On the next weekend, we went out hunting again. This time, I was bundled up in my ridiculous space outfit. We went back to the same area. I picked my own spot and Chet went on ahead. I stood with bated breath for what seemed to be hours. I was sort of daydreaming, or staring off into space, when right before my eyes a buck emerged from under a pine tree. His head was lowered and his nose was practically touching the ground. As he came nearer, I waited like Chet had taught me, until he came as near as he probably was going to get. I raised the gun, peered into the sights, aiming at the grayish brown coat in the chest section. Wham! I shot him.

He stopped for a second. I waited for him to fall but he jumped over the stone wall. I watched him leap over some fallen logs and that was the last I saw of him. Chet came up along the wall. I told him that the buck laid just over the log. I was sure that I had gotten him.

Chet said, "Show me exactly where you stood." When we got there, Chet squinted and said, " Come on." We walked to a tree that was about 4 or 5 inches wide. There was a bullet mark that went right into the tree. I had several trees between me and the deer. I was teased a lot for killing more trees than a woodsmen could kill in one season. But all that didn't discourage me. I kept on hunting with all my silly outfits. I think the deer came out each time just to see me. Many times, they would come dangerously close to get a look.

Once when I was out hunting, another hunter came by. He saw me and got real curious about my outfit. He said: " I'll be damned! It's a woman."

As you could probably guess, I turned out to be quite the hunter. I saw plenty of deer but more often than not, I shot off their hair, hit several trees, or just plain old missed them altogether. Now and then, the cartridge would flip out of the clip right after I shot the gun. But the deer kept coming.

The next year, Chet bought me a new gun for Christmas. It was a 35 Remington. I bought a new red down quilted insulated outfit, hand warmers and insulated boots. I had the works! I was more determined than ever to get a buck. Well, I still saw some deer but I think I looked like something that they had seen before. The whole darn family never did turn out to look at me again. By that time, I, too, had changed. I liked my open sight on the gun which helped me to stop shooting the trees.

Finally I did it. I shot my first buck. I was pretty proud when Chet, after hearing only two shots, came up to find me with a dead deer. I already had it gutted and was ready to head back to the camp. Everyone thought I would stop hunting after that. I was going to feel sorry for the deer and never go out again. I proved them all wrong. It was just the opposite. I had the hunting bug and now I liked hunting more than ever. Now, I was going to be out there on opening day and I'd keep hunting until I shot a deer. For two years in a row, it took me until the last few days of hunting season to get that buck. Sometimes, I had to go out alone. Chet had to work but I managed to find other people, like my son-in-law and his friends. They were kind enough to take me along. I never minded steep mountains or the deep snow, as long as I was hunting. Also, I never shot at anything that was moving. As a matter of fact, I think I waited too long for some deer to get a little closer.

I never liked hunting close to other people. I had very little patience when they sneezed, moved, coughed, or took a deep breath. Chet always said: " She sure keeps quiet when she's hunting." Then he added: "That's really the only time she is quiet!" Maybe, he doesn't realize that I'm frozen that way.

If I don't have anyone to go hunting with, I just go by myself. It was not uncommon for me to get a deer all by myself. After hauling it for a while, I would usually come across someone who would help me. One thing I did learn was that just because there wasn't any sign of blood, doesn't mean that you didn't hit the deer.

One time, I hit a young buck. He took off running. I picked up the tracks and followed him. I noticed that his hoof marks dragged more and more as they went along. Then, looking up over a rise under a low pine tree, I spotted his head. The buck had laid down and was looking up the valley where he could hear the voices of other hunters that were on a drive. But he didn't see me. I shot and got him right through the neck. I waited until after his sharp hooves had stopped lashing out for good. I gutted him out, got out my nylon strap, put the liver into a plastic bag and got him to the car.

I remember one time last year when Chet and I were coming home from hunting all day, I spotted a 10-pointer standing about 150 yards off the road.

I said: " Stop the car! There's a deer in the woods."

We got out of the car and walked toward the shoulder of the road. We scoped our eyes through the woods and sure enough, there he was. I fired one shot and he was dead. What a beauty! He weighed about 190 pounds all dressed out. The head is staring down on me right now. Every time I see it, it makes me long for hunting season.

It was quite common in those days for a man to say: "Boy, if my wife would take to hunting and hunt with me, I'd be the happiest man in the world." So go, gals. You too could get bit by the hunting bug and then you'd look forward to the cold, snow, and deer season. My Chet doesn't complain when he comes home from work and there isn't any supper ready during hunting season. I can always say: "You asked for it. It was you who started me hunting."

Of course, gals, the woods could stand some modern plumbing conveniences, or even if they weren't modern. Just a place to go would have been fine. So be careful, gals. Don't wear white underwear that resembles a deer flag or you may end up having the hunting bug shot right out from under you.

One day I asked Chet what he thought of having a wife who likes to hunt? Adding is it good or bad?

After thinking for a few minutes he said: "Well, I like it. We both enjoy it so much but it's my sport and I'll be darned if I like to be told: 'You just don't see deer, you're too noisy, and you move too much.'

"I will admit that you see a lot more deer but I don't have so many bullets scarring trees that come between me and the deer. But I do think that having a wife who enjoys hunting is pretty darn good, and to have her enjoy cooking and eating the game is great. But stop trying so damned hard to outdo me like a hound dog on a scent. You just never give up. You keep me pooped out from opening day to closing day. I'm glad that I have to go to work part of the time to rest up."

Then he ended by saying: "Say, how about going north this fall, as soon as their season opens up, as our season opens later down here. Maybe we can get in a longer season, Huh?"

About the Author

Randy was born and raised in Eagle Mills, New York. He loves fishing, hiking, photography, and walking around unique villages in the Adirondacks, Vermont, and Massachusetts. He has so many hobbies that he's never bored with life and he spends a lot of time at his family camp at Raquette Lake.

He is the current president of the Friends of Grafton Lakes State Park and also a member of the FFLA (Forest Fire Lookout Association) which helps to save fire towers throughout the state of New York and the country.

Randy currently works for the Brunswick Central School District having served on the maintenance staff for 24 years. In the past, he has served as a volunteer fire fighter for the Center Brunswick Volunteer Fire Company, the Eagle Mills Volunteer Fire Department, and the Grafton Fire Company.

Order these books by Marty Podskoch

Podskoch Press has a variety of books about the history of the Adirondack and Catskill regions. *The Adirondack Stories: Historical Sketches I and II* tell interesting stories through the comic sketches of Sam Glanzman, well known *DC Comics & Outdoor Life* illustrator. The Fire Tower books tell photo-illustrated stories that Marty researched throughout the region, which led to the development of his Adirondack CCC Camps book detailing the area's growth after the great depression. These are wonderful books for those who love the region's history. **Order yours today!**

Adirondack Stories, Historical Sketches	$18.95
Adirondack Stories II, 101 More Historical Sketches	$18.95
Two-Volume set Adirondack Stories (includes Volumes I & II)	$34.95
Fire Towers of the Catskill: Their History and Lore	$20.00
Adirondack Fire Towers:	
Their History and Lore, the Southern Districts	$20.00
Adirondack Fire Towers:	
Their History and Lore, the Northern Districts	$20.00
Adirondack Civilian Conservation Corps Camps:	
History, Memories, and Legacy of the CCC	$20.00

Prices do not include shipping and postage. Call or write for total price.
Order these autographed books from:

43 O'Neill Lane, East Hampton, Connecticut 06424
podskoch@comcast.net 860-267-2442